Patience

written by
Zanni Louise
art by
Missy Turner

FIVE MILE

Hi, I am Jack.
My name is Lila!
Hola, I am Mina.

I am Li Wei.

I'm Rosie ...

... and this is Freckles!

A big heart helps you care for the world, care for yourself, and care for others.

But how do you grow your heart? One ingredient you can use to grow your heart is patience.

What is patience?

There are lots of reasons why patience is important ...

Patience is learning to wait.

Mina has been seven *forever.*

'When am I eight?' she asks her mum. 'Tomorrow? The next day?'

'Only two weeks away!' says Mum.

Two weeks? That's way too long!

Mina makes a list to keep herself busy:

Make costumes.
Practise circus tricks in the backyard.
Draw invitations.

Mina discovers waiting for her party is also fun!

Learning something new isn't always easy. Building your patience muscles helps.

Jack is learning a new magic trick.

The coin keeps slipping. His fingers tie in knots.

Jack takes a deep breath in and breathes out.

He remembers other things that were hard at first. Like reading, swimming and playing guitar.

He has to be patient and practise one movement at a time.

Soon, Jack can pull a coin out
from Mina's ear!

Sometimes things are so exciting that patience feels impossible!

Rosie's aunt, Clara, has a new baby, Willow.

Rosie can't play with the baby until Willow is bigger.

Rosie tries to pay attention to all the lovely things about Willow as a baby.

She smells like milk.

She's soft like velvet.

She sounds like a kitten.

Rosie knows that growing takes time. So does learning to be a big cousin!

Slowing down and practising patience can make you feel calmer. You might even notice new things.

The new pool has finally opened. Li Wei can't wait!

'No running!' says the lifeguard. 'It's dangerous!'

Li Wei slows down.

He notices the hot ground. The kids dressed in matching dragon suits. The new diving board.

Finally ...

Splash!

The water feels amazing.

Patience is being respectful. It's a way of showing others you care.

Lila's so excited to tell her parents about her Show and Tell.

But they are busy talking.

Lila is a bubble that is about to burst!

She imagines herself floating, which makes her feel calmer.

Lila remembers how much she liked it when her classmates listened respectfully to her Show and Tell.

'Thank you for waiting, Lila,' says Mum. 'Come sit with me and tell me all about your day.'

Being patient gives you the chance to spend time with others.

Jack is first to finish his spaghetti. 'Can I go and play?' he asks.

'Please wait until everyone's finished,' says Jack's dad.

Jack's wriggly. All he wants to do is kick a ball.

But listening to the adults makes Jack realise how nice it is spending time with Grandad and Grandma.

Finally, Grandad puts his cutlery together.

'Do you want to kick a ball with me, Grandad?' asks Jack.

Sometimes you need to be patient with yourself. And forgive yourself for making mistakes.

Li Wei can't open his old music box.
He tugs. He bangs. He wrestles.

POP!

The music box opens, but not the way Li Wei wants. Oh no!

Li Wei is mad at himself for being so impatient.

He breathes in. Breathes out.

Mistakes happen. Next time, Li Wei will try to be more careful.

For now, his music box makes a perfect insect home.

Sometimes you need to be patient with others. It helps to imagine how someone else might be feeling.

Rosie's dog, Freckles, has been naughty lately. She even destroyed Rosie's favourite skates!

'Stop, Freckles!' cries Rosie.

Then Rosie imagines how Freckles is feeling about all the changes that are happening.

Rosie has been spending lots of time with her new baby cousin. Maybe Freckles is lonely.

Rosie decides to spend extra special time with Freckles. She even gets Freckles her own toy!

Good things can happen when you are patient.
Not just for you, but also for others.

The friends have been waiting for the bus forever! It's stuck in traffic, which means they might be late to the circus.

Jack is fidgety.
Rosie is jumpy.
Li Wei's disappointed.
Lila scrunches her ticket
and kicks the gravel.

Mina, though, is enjoying spending time with her friends. She starts to sing. The others join in. Singing helps pass time.

Everyone on the bus sings all the way to the circus.

Learning patience can be tricky. But when you practise and build your patience muscles, it helps you

learn new things,

show others you care,

slow down and feel calmer.

Feeling calm helps you enjoy things you might not have noticed before.

Patience helps your heart grow so you can look after the world, yourself and each other.

Can you think of times you've needed patience?

Let's talk about self-belief

Can you think of a time when you needed to be patient?

Venita meditator

'I like to set goals in my life. But sometimes they take so long to achieve and I have to be patient with myself. It can feel hard at the time, but I know being patient will be worth it in the end.'

Ant teacher

'It can be hard to be patient, especially when the world isn't moving as fast as me. I try though. To me, patience is about kindness, respect, slowing down and often, being uncomfortable. When I feel impatient, I remind myself that we all have different ways of operating and my needs are no more important than anyone else.'

Richard electrician

'I'm rewarded daily when I'm patient. As an electrician, I sometimes have to climb into a roof to retrieve a cable. I have to be especially patient to reach it safely!'

Mandy teacher, author & illustrator

'My sister was really talented. She could sing like a magical bird, make up songs, play piano like Mozart and draw anything she wanted to draw! I had to work super hard and keep trying to grow my skills ... But guess what? Now I'm a music teacher and an illustrator.'

Discussion questions for children

Patience is staying calm and learning to wait, which can be hard if it's something you really want!

- Can you think of a time in the last few days when you had to wait?
- What feelings did you notice in your body while you were waiting? Did you have jumpy feet, wiggly fingers, tight shoulders, hot cheeks or butterflies in your tummy?
- Can you name the emotions that went with those body feelings? Were you bored, annoyed, frustrated, nervous or excited?
- What did you do while you were waiting? What could you try next time, to help you be more patient?
- Who helps you strengthen your patience muscles?

Notes for parents and carers

Patience is our ability to manage feelings like frustration, boredom and excitement, so we can cooperate with others and achieve our goals.
For children, it may involve waiting for something they want, persevering with a difficult task, listening to others or waiting their turn. A child's abilities to wait and control their impulses has been linked to a range of positive outcomes later in life. It's okay to feel impatient sometimes, but we need to learn how to cope with emotions in healthy ways.

Some children find it quite easy to be patient, whereas others are more impulsive and need lots of support. Patience is also more difficult when a child is tired, hungry, unwell or in an unfamiliar situation. If a child feels anxious they may be irritable and reactive, and need help from their caregivers to slow down. Patience also depends on a child's developmental stage. Toddlers find it very difficult to wait and need lots of distraction. In the preschool years, and into primary school, self-regulation improves as children start to understand the benefits of patience.

Tips for nurturing patience in children

- Show your child how to be patient by managing your own emotions in challenging situations. Talk them through how you feel and what you are doing to stay calm.
- If you lose patience, be kind to yourself. Explain to your child that everyone struggles with patience, even adults, and we all make mistakes. If you have been impatient with your child, take the time to apologise and reconnect.
- Notice when your child is becoming frustrated, bored or overexcited. Acknowledge that waiting is hard and let them know you're okay with big feelings. Be present with them during difficult moments, while reminding them of the boundaries.
- Waiting is an opportunity to add to your child's toolbox of patience skills. Encourage them to use strategies like focussing on the breath, doing a quiet activity like reading, or noticing specific things in the room. Setting a timer can help give clear boundaries around an undefined waiting time.
- When your child is patient, reward the behaviour with descriptive praise, warmth and positive attention. If they make a mistake, remind them they are still learning to be patient and can try again next time.
- Ensure your expectations are appropriate for the situation, your child's age and their temperament. It may not be realistic for them to wait half an hour for dinner at a restaurant, and you may need to give them a snack or activity while they wait.
- Be predictable, consistent and follow through on your promises. If you need your child to wait 10 minutes, keep your eye on the time and try to stick to it. If you need more time, explain this clearly and tell them how much longer they need to wait.
- Find opportunities to practise patience in daily life, like cooking, gardening, hand-washing, tying shoelaces, doing up buttons, throwing, catching, kicking, climbing, building or learning to ride a bike. Games and imaginative play are also great for developing patience, turn-taking and cooperation.
- Give your child space to solve problems and experiment with different strategies when learning something new. Let them know you are there to help, if they need it.

Dr Ameika Johnson Child Clinical Psychologist

Also available in this book series

Made with love by the team at

FIVE MILE

Alex, Niki, Rocco, Graham, Jacqui, Claire & Sarah

Five Mile,
the publishing division
of Regency Media
www.fivemile.com.au

First published 2022

A catalogue record for this book is available from the National Library of Australia

Printed in China 5 4 3 2